FROM CHARCOAL TO DIAMOND

DISCOVER THE GREATNESS IN YOU!

1233

Brenda L. Caldwell, Ph.D.

Memphis, TN | www.unlimitedlifepublishing.com

BRENDA L. CALDWELL, PH.D.

ISBN-10:
0692993479

ISBN-13:978-0692993477 (Unlimited Life Publishing)

DEDICATION

I dedicate this book to my mother, Ruth Parker, who has always believed in me and encouraged me to pursue my dreams. Thank you for teaching me to give my best in everything I do and for your unwavering support. I also dedicate this book to my beloved grandfather, the late Lyles Caldwell, Sr., known by his family as "Dad." His influence on my life greatly shaped me into the person I am today.

BRENDA L. CALDWELL, PH.D.

ACKNOWLEDGEMENTS

First and foremost, I am thankful and grateful to God for empowering me to write this book.

I would also like to thank some special people in my life that helped birth this book from beginning to end. To my childhood friend, author Alice Faye Duncan Thompson, thank you for planting the seed in me years ago that I should write a book. You kept saying, "BC, just write, and the book will come."

To DeeDee Knowles, who is family to me and who is also my daily "Barnabus", thank you for your unwavering support and priceless encouragement as I worked on this book. To my sister, Lisa Parker, thank you for your constant words of encouragement as I wrote this book. To Kimmie West, thank you for being my proofreader and personal prayer intercessor. To author Dorothy Miller, Esq., thank you for editing the first three chapters of the original draft. To my W.O.W. Sister

Chiquita McGhee, thank you for a phenomenal job on the cover design.

To all my family and friends, I can't mention each of you by name, but I thank you from the bottom of my heart for believing in me.

FROM CHARCOAL TO DIAMOND

BRENDA L. CALDWELL, PH.D.

CONTENTS

BRENDA L. CALDWELL, PH.D.

FROM CHARCOAL TO DIAMOND

BRENDA L. CALDWELL, PH.D.

INTRODUCTION

I wrote this book so that you will be impacted by the truth that no matter what has happened in your life...greatness is in you! This is not just another inspirational book.

It is purposely compact and interactive, so that you will be encouraged, empowered, and enlightened with practical ways to maximize your life. Though it does not consist of many pages, if you open your heart you will receive more than you ever thought. Weaved throughout this book are affirmations and insightful nuggets that you will definitely be able to apply to your life.

My passion for writing this book is to inspire you to fully pursue your destiny and purpose despite where you are in life. You have so much on the inside of you, and I want to empower you to discover the true greatness that lies within you. I will be sharing with you an analogy of how a piece of coal is transformed into a diamond and how this relates to your life. I will also be sharing with you my personal story of being transformed from coal to diamond. I too have experienced the heating, cutting, and refining that happens in this process.

When writing each chapter of this book, I thought about those who needed to be reminded not to let the grave have their gifts, talents, and dreams. I thought about those who have struggled with feelings of self-doubt, insecurity, fear, rejection, or anger. I thought about those who have had their hearts and dreams broken. I thought about those who have been affected by the power of words. I thought about those who need to discover their true value and worth. I thought about those who need to realize the gift of being themselves and making a difference doing so. I thought about those who have continued to delay their destiny by putting things off. I thought about those who, despite outer appearances, are struggling with inner turmoil. I thought about those who have been waiting for a long time for a breakthrough. I thought about those who needed to hear and read words of encouragement and hope. I thought about those who want to shake off their past so that they can *be* more, *do* more, and *achieve* more in life.

If you're reading this book, I thought about you! Trust me. As your life coach, at certain points it will be as if I am speaking directly into your ear. This book contains words of life just for you! It is my belief that as you open your spirit, the words on these pages will uplift you, inspire you, and empower you to bring forth the true diamond that lies within you.

CHAPTER 1

SOME THINGS REALLY DO HAPPEN FOR A REASON

If you've ever doubted yourself, made excuses, felt fear, suffered heartache, experienced a painful setback, or wondered if any good could come out of a bad situation...then you're reading the right book. If you've ever wondered about your purpose, destiny, potential, value to others, or the legacy you will leave—again, you're reading the right book. If you've ever wanted to fully develop into the person you were born to be, you're definitely reading the right book at the right time in your life.

You see, everyone wants his/her life to count for something, and it is true that there is a divine purpose for every life. From baker to banker, janitor to judge, deliveryman to doctor, trash sweeper to teacher, we're all here for a reason. Job titles are only a small part of it.

You were born to make a difference. I know you've heard this before, but for the first time in your life, allow this statement to truly register on the inside of you. *You were born to make a difference.* You may have read other inspirational books, but in this book, you will experience something different. You will hear the life coach in me speaking into your ear. As you journey through, you will discover the essence of your worth and value as a person *packaged for a purpose* and *wrapped for a reason.* You will not only be inspired by words of life, but the book will come alive with simple yet life-changing empowerment tools that you will be able to apply for a lifetime.

In saying this, do you know that your life is destined to touch hundreds, if not thousands, of other lives? No matter who you are, you're your background is, who your parents are, what kind of childhood you had, or whether you have a college degree or no degree, your life counts! In fact, people who you don't even know yet are waiting for you to fully take hold of this truth because they need what is in you. Again, your life counts!

Do you realize that everyday, by the way you live, you're writing a book? There are chapters upon chapters being written, but one day someone else will stand up to give the summary of your book. This is called a eulogy. What you do now with your time, talents, gifts, money, energy, knowledge, failures, and disappointments will determine how you will be remembered and the legacy you leave.

What you've experienced in your life is for a reason. What you've overcome in life is for a reason. What you're going through right now is for a reason. What may be breaking you now is for a reason. And what you have on the inside of you that causes you to get back up every time life knocks you down is for a reason. Why? It's because greatness is in you!

There are so many people who don't believe this. One reason is that society has framed our minds to think based on social status, economic status, and physical status. In other words, we've been lead to believe that unless you're highly educated, in possession of lots of money, or have great looks, you're not that valuable. But this is not true. Who we are is not based on what we own, drive, or possess outwardly. It's who we really are on the inside that matters most in life. Not everyone is born to *do* the same thing, *be* the same thing, or *look* the same. The question is, "What do you have *in* you by way of gifts, talents, and passion that someone else needs right now or will need later?"

BROKEN DEAMS

Some years ago, in my last semester of working on my undergraduate degree in communications, I experienced agony over a decision. I was stressed out, but not because of grades or the fear of not graduating. My dilemma had to do with choosing between three major doors of opportunity. Door number one was whether to accept an assignment in Ghana, West Africa, as a two-year Peace Corps volunteer. I wanted to experience the once in a lifetime opportunity of serving and living in Africa. It thrilled me to think of doing this.

Door number two was the opportunity to accept a dream job as a reporter for a television station in Jackson, MS. This was a golden opportunity for someone coming straight out of college. I loved television and had already excelled in my internships to prepare for a television journalist career.

And then there was door number three: whether to accept the invitation of my college sweetheart (whom I believed to be my soon-to-be fiancé) to move to the same city his new career was taking him. He didn't want to go to Africa or Jackson, MS.

So, confident that we would get married, I chose door number three, only to have my heart broken three months later when we broke up. Just like that, with no real explanation, he walked out of our relationship, leaving me feeling devastated, rejected, and broken on the inside. Through my tears I kept thinking, *How could he walk out of my life after I gave up my dreams for him?*

For the next six months, I was depressed, unemployed, and angry. I could not understand why this had happened to me. What had gone wrong?

How did I go from being on top of the world with three great doors to choose from, to being unemployed, depressed, and brokenhearted? But I finally realized that self-pity had to be evicted; the bills still had to be paid.

Getting Back Up

After finding just enough strength to pick myself back up, I began intensely looking for a job in my field. There were no openings. I kept searching the want ads and sending out tapes to television stations, but it was like a door had slammed shut and the window of opportunity had closed tight. But, *finally*, I did land a job.

It wasn't with a television station. It was in telemarketing. I suddenly found myself making calls to grouchy customers eight hours a day trying to sell them a new long-distance service. I hated it! I kept thinking, *How in the world did I end up here?* I just couldn't understand how I had gone from having dream opportunities right at my doorstep to landing somewhere that barely paid minimum wage and brought much stress and shame.

You see, being the first one in my family to graduate from college, I wanted everyone to be proud of me. After all, the purpose of going to college is to have more opportunities to be successful in life. I kept thinking, *God, why are you doing this to me?* I was really feeling like a failure everyday, especially when I talked to college classmates who had already started their careers in their chosen field and were making good money.

Pressing Through to Get Through

Before long, depression began to creep back in. No one knew it. I kept a smile on my face. Some days I had to force myself to go to work.

If you've ever worked in sales, you know that it can be a stressful numbers game, filled with pressure to meet daily sales quotas.

Still hurting from the pain of being rejected by my ex, I dreaded going to work and facing the feeling of rejection every time I called a customer to sell them on our long-distance service, only to hear the words, "No, I'm *not* interested." I took this personally, even to the point of tears many days. Being told no so many times only compounded my feelings of rejection and frustration.

One particular day, my co-worker and friend Stacy, with whom I carpooled, talked me into "playing hooky." She hated working there almost as much as I did. So after arriving for work, we decided to leave the parking lot to head to the park for a day of fun. Just when we thought we were safe, our supervisor came rolling past us, smiling and waving as she headed in to work. Like sad little girls, Stacy and I knew at that moment our "play day escape" would not happen.

I also remember the "prison feeling" I had every time I needed a restroom break. I had exactly three minutes to be back from the ladies' room before my computer would log me out. In other words, every minute of my day was accounted for, even for the most personal of business I needed to attend to. I was miserable. But after about eight months, I realized that for some reason, I was supposed to work there.

Birthing Destiny

Almost every day, I found myself passionately encouraging different co-workers to pursue their dreams. In fact, word started getting around about me; before I knew it, people on my job who needed encouragement or a word of inspiration would seek me out. Lifting the spirits of others with words of life came so natural to me that I didn't know it was a gift.

I will never forget a co-worker, Debra, who came up to me one Friday afternoon with tears in her eyes. She grabbed me and thanked me for inspiring her to pursue her dream of going back to school. Debra had long desired to finish her college degree, and nearly everyday for about two months I encouraged her to go back. I remember telling her to visualize herself holding her degree in her hand. She was truly sincere in wanting me to know the difference I had made in her life. It humbled me to see her tear and to feel her gratitude.

A Divine Moment

Another special moment occurred at my telemarketing job when I "counseled" a customer to the extent of breaking a company policy. You see, my computer automatically dialed up Donna, a lady who lived in Dallas. When I gave her my usual spill to sell her on our long-distance service, she started yelling that she didn't make any long-distance calls and, therefore, didn't need our service.

But there was something in her voice that prompted me to find out the *real* reason. Upon talking with her through my lunch period, she confided in me that she was adopted and her husband was estranged from his family.

She told me that it was the first time she had admitted being adopted to anyone other than her husband. Listening to her, I could tell she was emotionally scarred by not knowing her birth parents. We bonded over the phone that day and even exchanged personal contact information, which was totally against company policy. I felt in my heart that God had assigned me to encourage her and help her work through the issues of being adopted.

After nearly a year of letter-writing and phone calls, Donna and her husband sent me an airline ticket to visit their family in Dallas. She said I had made a difference in her life, and she just had to meet me in person. I was nervous about going, mainly because my mother said that Donna could be "crazy." You know how protective mothers can be. But I went anyway and had an awesome time. We talked a few more times after my visit. Then, just like that, the assignment was over.

Destiny Has Dues

The experiences with Debra and Donna and several other co-workers spoke volumes to me. I realize that I was divinely placed in this telemarketing job. Looking back now, I'm thankful for the opportunity to go through this season of training to do what I was born to do as a professional speaker and life/dream coach.

Incredibly, I worked at this company three years to the exact date. With a college degree, my pay was still only $6.25 per hour plus commission. It's called paying dues. But what I gained from working there proved to be more priceless than any paycheck.

Though it's not the path I would have chosen, looking back I'm grateful for this divine placement. I now understand the reason. It was the birthing place for my gifts to be practiced and nurtured. I did eventually work part-time in the television industry for a few years. But the circumstances of landing at my telemarketing job gave birth to my destiny. Discovering my ability to penetrate people's hearts with words of encouragement, exhortation, and inspiration was a revelation that I had something on the inside of me that was indeed valuable to others.

The Reason Will Be Revealed

It's amazing how what seems like the worst thing that could happen
turns out to be the best thing for you. Though I couldn't see it at the time, God could see that Mr. Wrong would never have valued my gifts enough to nurture them; he no longer saw real value, worth or potential in me. Now I know that his rejection was God's protection!

You may also have had some painful experiences in your life that to this day you don't understand. But, believe me—it's for a reason. You may have experienced the heartache of broken dreams or broken relationships.

There's a reason, and it *will* be revealed.

You may be in a situation right now that is painful. If so, I'm sure you feel frustrated, fragmented, and fatigued just thinking about it. You may also feel stressed, stretched, or strained by the pressures of having to deal with this day-in and day-out.

Like me, you may be wondering, "Why am I going through this?" I know it's tough, but trust me—there's a reason beyond what you see or feel right now. You won't break. You won't wither. You won't give up. You will get through it because there is much more in store for you!

As your life coach, I want you to start encouraging yourself daily by speaking the following affirmation aloud until you can feel these words coming alive on the inside of your heart:

This will not break me! I am more than a conqueror! Something good will come out of this because I have a destiny!
(If the above affirmation doesn't apply to you right now, just keep reading. There's one designed just for you! When you read the one that fits you, start speaking it everyday.)

You have the power and the strength to press through anything to get to your place of destiny. The seed of destiny is being developed in you right now. This means what God created you to *be* and to *do* to leave your own mark on the world is being molded in you. You have something in you that will make the world around you a better place. Destiny means you have a place and a position of divine influence just because you were born to make an impact in this area. In other words, there's a divine plan for your life to touch others in some way. More will be revealed to you later about how to discover your divine assignment and position of power.

Whatever you happen to be naturally gifted at, you're being molded in ways that you never even thought possible. You've only scratched the surface of using your God-given abilities. Like a coal miner who goes far below the surface in search of pebbles with potential, stop scratching and start digging. You might not be there today, but you're on your way! You have a lot more on the inside of you that needs to come out, and there are also some things that still need to be put in you. There's something for you to discover about your gifts, talents, strengths, abilities, and character that will shape you for your destiny.

Learn the Lesson

Remember: wherever you are in your life right now, it's for a reason. Don't despise it. Don't reject it. Don't run from it. Whatever God wants you to learn now will greatly benefit you later. Don't even try to figure out why you're going through this. Just know that God has a master plan. He knows better than you what you need to help develop the character and strength to walk out your destiny. Let's look closer at the word *destiny*. You will see the word *tiny*. However, there is nothing tiny about becoming all that God created you to be. On your journey, there will be lessons that will turn into blessings.

Family and friends may not know what to say or do for you right now. It's actually a blessing; there are some life lessons that you just have to go through to get to where God is truly taking you. So don't let anyone rescue you. Sometimes being rescued causes you to miss the lesson. You'll have to take the test again. This only delays your destiny. Don't reject the lesson. It may not *look* good or *feel* good, but if you stay the course, it will only produce a greater purpose in your life.

Here's an affirmation for you to say aloud if this applies to you. Repeat it until you feel these words coming alive on the inside of you.

What I'm going through right now is working for my good.
If you didn't say the above affirmation aloud the first time, give it a try. You will feel the power of hearing yourself speak these words of life.

This book is entitled *From Charcoal to Diamond* for a reason. Right now where you are in life may be like a piece of coal...seemingly not worth much value at all. But just keep reading. In the next chapter, I'll begin sharing with you this powerful process of how charcoal becomes a diamond and how it relates to your life. For now, remember: sometimes things will happen in your life that will ultimately be for your *good,* your *growth*, and will lead you to your *greatness.*

BRENDA L. CALDWELL, PH.D.

CHAPTER 2

A COAL'S NIGHTMARE, A DIAMOND'S DREAM

It all begins with carbon atoms. While carbon doesn't excite very many of us, the mention of diamonds makes our ears and our eyes pop. Expensive, shiny, and delicately crafted, diamonds have long had the mass appeal as the premiere jewelry for those with exquisite taste. The most precious of gems, diamonds, at one time, were just chunks of coal.

The next time you barbecue, take a close look at the charcoal. You'll see some tiny fragments mixed in the burnt wood and carbon atoms. Before you throw away the ashes, take note that these same used-up coals have the ultimate potential of turning into diamonds. In fact, the very pencils we use to write with are made of these same carbon atoms.

Just as a side note to men, don't even think about trying to pull a pencil or a piece of charcoal off as a "potential diamond" for your wife. It just won't work. Not enough pencils or charcoal chunks could be packed up, fixed up, or gift-wrapped that could earn the right to be called "a girl's best friend." But long before a diamond can become a girl's best friend, it must go through an intense process of transformation.

these First of all, it is mind-blowing to me that coal miners risk their lives on a daily basis to search the depths of the earth in mines to preserve potential jewels. Their search can take days, weeks, or months before anything of substance can be found. But it's worth the search; the potential payoff in discovering highly valuable diamond gemstones is worth thousands of dollars.

In the Heat of the Moment

It is remarkable how a piece of coal made of carbon and burnt wood pieces becomes something so beautiful and treasured. To become a diamond, coal must first undergo great amounts of pressure and heat. With the process of being put to continuous heat and extreme pressure, these carbon bonds inside the coal have no choice but to eventually press into the structure that forms a diamond.

But I'm sure if coal could speak before this transformation happens, it would scream, "Stop! I can't handle this heat and pressure. It's too much! It's not worth it!" If coal had feelings, it might say, "I don't *feel* like going through all of this! This is stressful, painful, and tiresome! I don't feel like working on myself anymore!" And if coal could write a friend, it might say, "Please come and rescue me! This is a nightmare! I'm being heated up everyday and pressured into becoming something different from what I am now. I just don't understand it. Please help me!"

If coal were you and I was your friend, I would not rescue you. Why? Because I know that no matter how you *feel* or how stressful, painful, or tiresome it may be right now, you're on your way to becoming a dream diamond.

Being Put to the Press

Sometimes we experience pain, hurt, and disappointment in a way that breaks our spirit. There are devastating things you may already have gone through or may go through at some point in your life.

When you're faced with issues such as loss of job, loss of loved one, divorce, unforgiveness, abuse, broken relationships, sudden illness, betrayal, or rejection, the pain can be almost unbearable.

It can leave you feeling, among other things, shocked, numb, angry, and confused. But remember, it's for a reason. Like carbon coal being put to the fire, you must be put to the press. You may want to run, scream, or turn the heat off. But, like I mentioned earlier, it's for your *good*, your *growth*, and will only lead you to your *greatness*.

Someone Is Watching You!

We hear a lot about the importance of maintaining a positive attitude in everything. But what exactly does the word *attitude* mean? Attitude is our response or reaction to life situations, circumstances, and events. Stuff happens. The question is, how do you react to it? Attitude is also your thoughts or feelings toward something in particular. It's not easy to maintain a positive attitude in every situation, but it is possible, with a conscious effort, to remember that *someone is watching you.* Have you ever stopped to realize just how much this statement is conveying? Someone is watching how you handle yourself when life throws you a curve ball. Thus, your attitude will make all the difference in determining the growth that will lead to your greatness.

I will never forget the thrill of finally being released from my telemarketing job. I answered a blind ad and before I knew it, I was working for a social service organization, making a difference working with youth. After one year, I received a promotion to director of a new food co-op program that the organization was starting up.

With this came the responsibility of hiring a staff, traveling out of town for training, planning, and developing the program from scratch. It was quite an undertaking that required long hours and hard work in order to get it going. Finally, the program was underway. It started off great with the excitement of being new. We had plenty of volunteers. But after about nine months, it was not doing well financially.

A Blow to the Soul

Have you ever experienced someone telling you something that you just weren't ready to hear? Most of us would probably call this being "caught off guard." Well, that's exactly how I felt the day my supervisor timidly knocked on my office door and stood at the entrance. She was obviously nervous about what she needed to say to me. Then, with one gasp of air, she said words I will never forget. "Brenda, we want to free you up. Connie will take over as director, as of tomorrow. We need you to be a field representative to simply go out and sell the program to the community."

My co-worker was replacing me as director? I was crushed. It hit me like a ton of bricks. Hurt and confused, all I could think about was the long hours and hard work I had put in to help get this program off the ground and how unfair it was to replace me. I felt the wound of rejection all over again, not to mention humiliation and embarrassment. *It was a blow to my soul.* This demotion left me with a wounded heart filled with anger and resentment. My attitude was not good at all.

In a desperate attempt to get my position back, I met with the president of the organization three times. But, it was to no avail. He didn't budge. All he would say each time was, "This is in the best interest of the organization." His words cut me deeply. I felt like the poster child for rejection. I also felt betrayed because I had given my all to this organization, working twelve-hour days and two weekends a month. In my mind, I just could not understand why I was suddenly receiving such unfair treatment. Although I felt I was being treated unfairly, I knew I had to make one of two choices: quit or change my attitude. I knew that the staff I had hired and our volunteers were watching me.

Don't Quit

It truly wasn't easy to do, but after praying for direction, I decided to push past my hurt feelings and stick it out. During my prayer time, I released the anger and frustration. Humbling myself, I shook off my feelings of resentment and embarrassment and accepted my new role as field representative. I decided to do this job to the best of my ability, even though my heart was not in it.

After dealing with this for several weeks, I finally chose to "get the chip off my shoulder" and look for the good in it. When I began to focus on being positive everyday, my outlook changed. I realized that I couldn't control what was happening, but I *could* control my attitude towards it. I consciously started displaying respect for the person who replaced me as director. I knew it was important to display the right attitude daily, no matter what I thought or felt. In fact, to help maintain the right attitude, I started saying a daily affirmation that to this day I still say.

Today is MY day. I'm expecting something good to come my way!

Demoted into Destiny!

I wasn't certain of the full meaning of the word *demoted* until checking with Webster for the writing of this book. However, I *was* sure of the feelings I had associated with this word. To be demoted means to be *reduced* in rank, grade, or position. This sounds bad unless God has a master plan for allowing you to experience a "divine demotion." Being reduced is not the end of the world. It can actually set your feet in motion to follow the blueprint originally drafted for your life.

You see, when I was in the field speaking on behalf of the organization, my daily confession slowly began to pay off. *Some good things did begin to come my way.* Doors of opportunity began to open for me. Others outside the organization took notice of me. I started receiving invitations to speak professionally and be paid for it. I was amazed. I didn't know people really got paid to share words of inspiration. I definitely didn't know I had something in me that people would pay for.

It's amazing how things work out for your good. Being demoted actually gave birth to my speaking career. In the process, it also helped to develop the qualities I would need in order to become successful in my work.

Blessed by the Fire

Like coal in the fire, I was heated up to burn the impurities of self-pity, anger, and resentment out of me. I was put to the press to bring forth the humility, patience, submission, and perseverance that would enable me to become the diamond I was created to be. I realize now that the day I was "freed up" by my supervisor was truly God's plan to position me to walk in the fullness of my destiny and purpose. What an awesome God who not only begins a good work in us, but brings it to completion!

Though it's been years, this was an invaluable life experience that has served me well. In fact, this same organization, having respect for the work I do today, sought me out a couple of years ago to do a major contract to present my abstinence program, Purity is Powerful® for their youth participants. The same person who replaced me as director contacted me regarding this project. It was an overwhelming success! God sweetly redeemed me. But this opportunity never would have opened up to me had I not accepted the challenge of being put to the press years earlier. I'm so thankful that I didn't quit.

Owning the Right Attitude

I shared this story to challenge you to maintain the right attitude as you go through your own press test. There is something that God wants to burn *off* and burn *out* of you that may be hindering you from being all that you were created to be. Whatever it is, be like *coal*—allow yourself to go through the fire. If you're struggling with a situation in your life that you feel is unfair or you just don't understand, deal with your feelings and check your attitude. Ask yourself, "What can I learn in this? How can going through this benefit me later? How can going through this help someone else?"

Like me, you may have experienced *a blow to your soul* that is hard to get over. Whatever it is, it doesn't have to destroy you or control you. Just because it caught *you* off guard doesn't mean that God was caught off guard. *Nothing* happens that God doesn't already have a plan for. He sees the end before we ever have to deal with the beginning. So no matter how you *feel*, if you deal with this in the right way, you will be blessed with peace, inner strength, and character development that will only help push you into the fullness of your destiny. However, God is patient. If you handle this situation the wrong way, it will only prolong your lessons to be learned, and you'll face this same test again until you pass it.

If you're in a similar situation right now, *don't quit*! This is a priceless experience that will pay off dividends for you later on. So, don't even be discouraged. Just like coal has to go through the fire to get the impurities out, so do you! The heat in your life is only burning some things out of you that need to come out and refining you on the inside. In fact, if you can think of some inner feelings that you know need to be burned away, take a moment to list them below. It's important to be honest with yourself.

_____

_____

_____

_____

_____

_____

Someone Is Watching You

It's so important to be honest with yourself because as I shared earlier, someone is watching you. Someone is watching how you handle tough situations. Someone is taking note of the attitude you display from day to day. The powerful thing about our attitude is that we can spread it like the common cold. Being negative can expose others to germs such as complaining, criticism, anger, bitterness, sarcasm, and jealousy. These "attitude germs" can easily rub off on those you come in contact with. Likewise, being positive has the power of spreading enthusiasm, encouragement, acceptance, support, and respect. This attitude will make all the difference in every situation. Choose, no matter how you feel, to approach life with a positive attitude. It will pay off!

Always remember that in tough situations, your attitude will either make it better or make it worse. Whatever challenges you're facing right now, don't run from them. How you handle yourself in situations that are difficult speaks volumes to those around you. Some circumstances will come into your life to bring out the best in you, so that in turn, you can help bring out the best in others.

Here's a daily affirmation that will help you maintain a positive outlook everyday. Say it aloud until you can feel the words coming alive on the inside of you.

Today, I choose *to have a positive attitude* no matter what *and I choose to look for the good in every situation today. My* attitude *will make a difference in someone else's life today.*

These life-giving words are powerful when truly spoken consistently out of your mouth. Changing your attitude will change your life.

Some people run from job to job, relationship to relationship, or one situation to another only to encounter the same problems. If this is you, open your heart to realize that the problem is with you. There's something in you that needs to come out so that the diamond in you can come forth. A coal's nightmare is a diamond's dream. Without going through the intense heating, cutting, and chipping process, a diamond will remain *in the rough*. Likewise, so that the diamond in you can come forth, you must undergo this same process. Things happen in life that sometimes hurt or anger, but your response will make all the difference in your ability to heal and grow from it. Therefore, as your life coach I challenge you to really examine your heart—be totally honest with yourself about any thoughts or feelings that you may be holding on to that need to be let go. It's time to let it go because you're on your way to greatness. So don't delay your own destiny.

In the next chapter, we will begin to examine those things that maybe hindering you from discovering the greatness that is truly in you.

BRENDA L. CALDWELL, PH.D.

CHAPTER 3

BROKEN, DAMAGED, CRACKED...BUT STILL VALUABLE

Although the most priceless of all gems, diamond gemstones do not look like much at all in their natural state. With a dull, grayish look and rough edges, the value of these potential jewels could easily escape the eyes of anyone other than a highly skilled diamond cutter.

In fact, the phrase "a diamond in the rough" stems from a metaphor for the original unpolished state of diamond gemstones, especially those that have the potential to become high-quality jewels.

Outer blemishes such as scratches, chips, or nicks can be removed in the cutting process. Inner flaws such as cracks, inclusions, or bubbles are more serious. Sometimes diamonds can be subjected to laser beams that will burn out a flaw and leave a barely visible hole.

We all have some outer blemishes that need to be cut way. If not tended to, these scratches, chips, or nicks will fail to show the value of who we really are. Outer blemishes are what others can see, such as a bad attitude, anger, or jealousy.

Inner flaws are those root causes of the outer blemishes such as unforgiveness, bitterness, insecurity, and rejection. Just as with gemstones, our inner flaws are serious and must be confronted with precision and purposefulness.

Victim No More!

Situations will wound us and *people* will wound us, whether intentional or unintentional. The flaws from these wounds can even affect your physical health if not dealt with properly. That's why it's important to talk to someone you trust about your feelings. Whatever is buried deep inside you will not die. It must come out. You'll be amazed at the weight that will lift off you just by expressing your feelings to someone you feel safe enough to open up to.

If you open your heart and your eyes, there is someone in your life who is willing to listen to you. If you can't find a person, try talking to God. He's always willing to listen. Once you have talked out your feelings, regardless of what they are, make a decision to let go of any pain, hurt, or disappointment you may be holding on to.

Even though it will take some time before your emotions catch up with your decision, you must let go of the past; lives are waiting to be touched by you in the future. There's someone in your life right now who needs what God has put in you.

You may have been abandoned, abused, neglected, rejected, ostracized, or traumatized, but you're not a victim! You may have been walked over, stepped over, and looked over, but you're not a victim! You may have even been put down, beaten down, or knocked down in life. You may have gone through life feeling unloved, unwanted, and unhappy. You may have made some messy mistakes in life. You may have grown up in an abusive home. You may have been abandoned by your mother or father. Even so, you're not a victim!

You may have suffered betrayal by a friend or family member. You may have been fired from a job or demoted. You may have gone through divorce, depression, or dejection. You may have had your name or character slandered. Still, you're not a victim.

How do I know? Because if you're reading this book, you're still alive! That means no matter what you've gone through in your past, it didn't kill you!

A diamond can be *broken*, *cracked*, or *damaged*; however, it is still valuable. No matter what has happened in life, you are still a person of incredible value. The heat of going through such intense fire will only develop you into the brilliant diamond you're destined to become. God will use every painful experience in your life to serve a purpose in someone else's life.

Take a Deep Breath and Let It Go

I shared with you in the first chapter the pain and rejection over whom I thought was "the one" walking out my life without an explanation. It took me a long time to get over this, simply because there had never been closure. But after about four years of carrying this baggage, one night I started opening up to a friend about my true feelings of anger, resentment, and rejection.

She didn't judge me. She just listened. It felt so good to finally express what I had been holding on to for years. My friend told me that I deserved to get it all out. "God has a purpose for allowing this and a greater plan for your life." Just hearing those words strengthened my soul and gave me the courage to finally let it go. I cried. I yelled. I vented from my soul.

A few days later, I made a conscious decision to do something else that I knew deep down I needed to do in order to move forward with my life. I decided it was time to forgive. I knew that forgiving was the only way my wounded heart would heal. Therapeutic healing basically means confronting someone without the person having to be present. It is a powerful technique
that really works. Picture this. I wrote his name on a piece of paper and placed it opposite me on the chair. Facing him therapeutically for the first time, as I looked at his name in the chair, I began to express as if he were in the room with me feelings I had held in. I said everything I felt I needed to say. Then, taking a deep breath, I spoke the following words out of my mouth, "Because I want to be set free, I *choose* to forgive you and I *choose* to let go of the hurt and pain your actions caused me."

The moment I said these words, I felt empowered as the emotional weights lifted off me. I felt peace fill my soul. It was freeing! After that day, I said this often during the next few weeks until I felt a total release in my heart that I had truly forgiven him.

Forgive and Be Free

Today, in my life-coaching role, I help others do what I had to learn to do myself. Do you need to be freed from any wrong feelings toward anyone in your life? If so, remember that forgiveness is a beautiful gift that you give to yourself as well as the person that has hurt you. It is also the only way you will be able to heal and move forward with your life. Unforgiveness is a *cancer* that eats away at your peace, joy, happiness, and ability to give or receive love as well as your destiny. If you're still holding any unforgiveness, resentment, or anger toward anyone, it's time to *choose* to let it go.

Remember, you can *live with it* or *deal with it.* Living with it hinders you. You have *too* much to do and are *too* valuable to *too* many other people to hold on to unforgiveness. It's not an emotion. It's a choice. If you're struggling with whether or not to make this choice, think for a moment how you have hurt someone and wanted to be forgiven.

In the same way that you want to receive the gift of forgiveness, you must give it away. There is no excuse for holding on to unforgiveness. Even if the person never admits to hurting you, you must forgive. If you never hear the words "I'm sorry," still you must forgive. It is a bridge to discovering your greatness. God has a master plan for your life. Pain can indeed give birth to a greater purpose. Today you can choose to forgive. It will release a power that will enable you to become all that God created you to be.

When you're ready, reach out to someone whom you trust to confide in or, as I said before, talk to God about your feelings. If you know in your heart that you need to let go of something or someone that has caused you hurt or pain, use therapeutic healing (like I did with the chair and slip of paper) because it is a practical exercise that really does work. Just get by yourself or with someone you feel very comfortable with. When you're ready to begin, start by saying the person's name, and then begin to express the feelings you have been holding in that caused your hurt and pain. Therapeutically, this person cannot deny your feelings or say anything that would cause even more hurt. This will empower you with strength and courage to express yourself like never before. Once you have said everything you've wanted and needed to say, take a deep breath and then make the following confession:

Because I want to be set free, I choose *to forgive you* [state person's name] *and I choose to release my feelings* [name your feelings and the situation]. *I know good will come out of this because I have a purpose and destiny. Therefore, I choose to let go of my feelings toward you as of this day* [state the date and year].

This may seem too simple to be effective. But trust me, it is powerful when you truly express from your soul. Often, people will tell you that you *need* to forgive, but don't tell you *how to*. I have used this technique several times over the years. It is both empowering and freeing.

Since this is an interactive book, you can stop to deal with this situation right now and pick the book up later, or you can wait until you've finished the book. But either way, if you need to deal with letting go of any wrong feelings toward someone, don't delay it; if you do, you'll only be delaying God's divine plan for your life.

Any unresolved issues or unhealed hurt in your heart will hinder you from being all you were created to be. Hiding pain, hurt, anger, and disappointment in your heart is stifling your health, emotional well-being, and your ability to bring good out of it. Life is too short and too precious to waste holding on to baggage. *Stop*! The last two paragraphs are very important. Please read them again.

What you've gone through is not in vain. Someone needs to hear you and be inspired by your strength and courage to get through it. There's a purpose for everything you have gone through. Indeed, someone needs to know your story.

Cut Like a Knife!

As your life coach, I want to empower and inspire you through my own life experiences in a way that helps you realize that everything you go through is only preparation for your destiny.

I can recall a time in my life when something pure became painful. I have loved basketball since I was about eight years old. As a star player all through junior and senior high school, I was determined to play in college. When I graduated from high school, I turned down scholarship offers out of town to try out as a walk-on for my hometown university. A walk-on is a player who tries out for a team with hopes of earning a scholarship. It was rough from day one. The coach treated me quite obviously different as a "walk-on" player.

If you ever watched the movie *Rudy*, you will appreciate this story all the more. *Rudy* is the true story of a young man who dreamed of playing football for Notre Dame all his life. Through blood, sweat, and tears, he made the team as a walk-on player, only to experience rejection by his coach. To this day, I cry whenever I watch this movie because I can so relate to Rudy.

I remember my feelings being hurt deeply on the second day of pre-camp when we had to run two miles around the track in scorching heat. The coach yelled out to a scholarship player running behind me, "Come on, Karen, run faster. Don't let the walk-on beat you!" Hearing this cut me like a knife but also fueled my energy. With tears in my eyes, I ran laps around that track as if it were the Olympic tryouts, proving that I deserved to be on the team. My determination paid off; I did make the team, but at the cost of breaking my spirit.

The coach had given me a positive evaluation for my play during the six-week pre-camp, but she cornered me the day before the regular season began to inform me that her loyalty was to her scholarship players first.

Seemingly, with as much sternness as she could muster up, she looked at me and said, "Brenda, there's a chance between slim and none that you'll ever play in a game, and an even slimmer chance that you'll ever travel with the team. But if you can accept these two conditions, I would love to welcome you as an official member of this basketball team." Hurt, confused, and yet strangely excited, I accepted these conditions with the hopes that she would change her mind.

Encourage Yourself!

I found out quickly that the coach would be a hard nut to crack. It was painful. She constantly reminded me that I was a walk-on with her
words, actions, and attitude toward me. One day, the assistant coach pulled me to the side to tell me that the coach was trying to make me quit. Since the coach had no confidence in me, it started to affect my self-esteem and self-confidence. Standing on the sidelines, I began to feel more like "a nobody" with each passing day. No matter how hard I practiced, I was a thorn in the coach's side. I could tell that she really didn't like dealing with me. Have you ever had the feeling that someone was only *tolerating* you rather than *appreciating* you? This is how I felt everyday in practice.

The joy of playing basketball was fading fast. I also felt inferior to the scholarship players. I found myself being very intimidated, especially whenever the star player was around. Though she seemed nice, looking back, I realize that I saw myself as a piece of worthless coal compared to her diamond status as the star of the team. I was really broken, damaged, cracked, and chipped, and most of all, I wanted to quit. It was hard feeling rejected and ignored by my coach, especially when all I wanted to do was contribute to the team.

To help boost my confidence, everyday before practice I started saying the phrase "Winners never quit and quitters never win. I'm a winner,
therefore, I won't quit!" The late Jimmy Valvano, former North Carolina State basketball coach, gave a stirring speech to his colleagues before he died. Referring to finding a cure for cancer, he told the audience, "Don't give up. Don't ever give up!"

I knew in my heart that I couldn't give up. I wanted to prove to myself that I could handle the coach's treatment and be better for it. With Coach Jimmy Valvano's message ringing in my ears, I decided to find a way to make myself valuable to the team, even if I never got off the bench to play at a home game or traveled with the team to an away game.

Using my natural ability to encourage and uplift others, I decided to become the best "cheerleader" from the bench I could be. During every home game, my voice would get hoarse from cheering very hard for my teammates, whether we were winning or losing. I didn't realize it then, but my motivational speaking gift was being developed as I continued to sit on that hard bench waiting for my chance to play.

Finally, half way through the season, because we were up by forty points, I finally got to play the last two minutes of a game for the first time, scoring my first and only two points of the season. My teammates were happy for me. The coach never said a word to me. I was so used to her treatment by then, it didn't bother me.

Valuable After-All

Through tears, prayers, and encouragement from the assistant coach, I survived that long season. I then decided to turn my attention to track the following year. Ten years after playing that one season of basketball, an amazing thing happened; my path crossed with my former star teammate. She had just moved back home after ten years of playing on a professional women's team overseas. It was good to see her, but I could tell there was something wrong with her.

She began to share how empty her life was without basketball. The more I listened, the more I understood why our paths crossed that day. I was no longer intimidated to be in her presence; my personal relationship with God had given my life real meaning and value.

After listening to her share her story, I began to do what I do best, offer words of encouragement. Then, with confidence and boldness, I asked my former star teammate would she like to invite the Lord into her life as personal savior. She said yes. In a single moment, I—the one who had felt like a nobody during my painful season on the team—was suddenly serving in a role of much greater importance in her life. She expressed gratitude from the bottom of her heart that winter day.

For me, it was as if God was saying, "Brenda, you may not have been valuable on the court, but you *were* valuable when it counted the most."

Two of the life lessons I learned from going through that experience is the importance of valuing everyone and treating people with dignity no matter who they are. I've since forgiven my old coach, realizing that she obviously had some issues that had nothing to do with me. Life is just too short to hold grudges. In addition, I've used this experience to help me in my own relationships with young people.

After college, as a volunteer, I coached boys' basketball for eight years at the Abe Scharf YMCA in Memphis. Thinking back on the hurtful feelings I had while sitting on the bench week after week in college, I made my policy to play

every player, whether we won or lost. Period! My teams
played for the league championship four times and won once. My players still keep in touch with me to this day. In the long run, winning in relationships is more important than winning on a court.

A True MVP!

So it is with you. No matter what you may have experienced in life that may have left you feeling rejected, God created you to win in life. Just like the dullness of gemstones in their natural state, what you've gone through may make you appear not worth much at all. But you are! Your life is invaluable to many whose lives you're destined to touch. Just like a precious gemstone, you may have been broken, damaged, and cracked, but you're still highly valued.

There are life lessons coming forth out of your own painful experiences. Embrace what you need to learn and realize that your life matters to someone who needs just what God has put in you. Like me, you may not be a star ballplayer, but you're definitely an MVP (most valuable player) to someone. Keep doing good unto others. Keep treating people right. Keep sharing your gifts and talents. Keep giving your best effort everyday! You may look like charcoal, but the truth is, you're a valuable diamond! Don't count yourself out just because some may not yet see the value in you.

On this note, it's time for another life-affirming word. Say the following aloud until you feel the words coming alive on the inside of you.

No matter what I've gone through, I'm a person of worth! I'm a winner! My life has value to others! Greatness is in me! (There's power in speaking it. As your life coach, I trust that you spoke this out of your mouth.)

You never know how your life will sometimes come full circle. Someone from your past may come into your life for a reason. If so, be willing to listen, encourage, pray for them, and help if possible. In doing so, you will reveal the diamond you really are just by being willing to *be* yourself and *give* of yourself.

CHAPTER 4

I DON'T RECEIVE THAT! DREAM BUILDERS
vs. DREAM BUSTERS

This chapter is very special to me. For years I've shared with people everywhere I go the power of spoken words. Now I'm excited about sharing this insight with you because I believe you have greatness in you that must be developed. This is why I want you to receive the revelation of the power of words as it relates to your dreams, your goals, and becoming the diamond you were born to be.

Words we have lived with, heard, and received into our spirit over the years have shaped us in some form or fashion. Speaking life or death is in the power of the tongue. Words can heal. Words can kill. Words can build up. Words can tear down. Words can lift your spirit. Words can break your spirit. Words can bless. Words can curse.

Did you know that *words* and *wind* have something profoundly in common? Let's compare them for a moment. You cannot *see* spoken words nor can you *see* wind. But you can *feel* the affects of both. Words and wind can push you forward or hold you back. The force of wind is so critical to an Olympic track athlete that it can make the difference between winning and losing a race. 100-meter athletes who have trained for years might still be hindered greatly at the start of a race if the wind is strongly blowing toward runners. Often when this happens, runners are slowed and records are not broken. Likewise, when the wind is blowing from behind, it helps to push the runners faster. Sometimes a record is broken for the fastest time because of the assistance of wind power.

Power of Words

Words have a similar power. Though unseen, there is a force of power within every word we speak. It is important to understand that words are the most creative force on the planet. Nothing happens until it is first spoken. There was no light until God said, "Let there be light." In the same way, our words have the power to speak things into existence. Whether positive or negative, words have the power to shape one's life. A person who constantly receives criticism would likely be afflicted with self-doubt and low self-esteem, among other issues. Likewise, a person who receives consistent encouragement and praise would likely have a healthier dose of self-confidence and self-esteem.

It's important to understand the connection of the brain, mouth, and ears that creates our words. The brain is like a computer. It stores everything it hears you speak, as well as what you receive into your inner spirit. Whatever you believe about yourself right now has a lot to do with the words you have heard, received into your spirit, and thus spoken out of your mouth. You have an outer ear that can be seen. But your inner ear is the spirit within you. I'll explain this more clearly a bit later.

Whoever started the phrase, "Sticks and stones may break my bones, but words will never hurt me," either didn't have a clue as to what they were saying or was in deep denial. The truth is that sticks and stones may break our bones, but words can break our spirit. Destructive words are like poison that gets into our blood stream and sucks the life out of us.

Dream Busters Only See Charcoal

When I was five years old, I remember being able to spell hippopotamus. (More than thirty years later, I admit I needed to use spell check.) The point is, I was a smart child! That is, until I entered first grade. just as if it were yesterday, I recall running into the classroom with the excitement in my little heart about the possibilities of learning new "big words." In less than 20 seconds, like a shot-down eagle, my spirit was broken when I heard my teacher yell the deathly words, "Sit down, dummy." Her words cut me like a knife. What had I done to make her call me a dummy?

Something on the inside of me shut down at that moment. I was psychologically paralyzed. I never got past that traumatic first day. I was called dummy nearly every day of my first grade year. Out of respect, I'd never mention her name. But, needless to say, I felt like worthless coal in her class. I was intimidated, fearful, and ashamed as though I had done something wrong. As a result, believing I was a dummy, I failed first grade and had to repeat it the following year. My mother enrolled me in a new school.

Dream Builders See the Diamond in You

This time an amazing bond happened on the first day of school. My new first grade teacher knew that I had failed the previous year. Her first words to me were, "Brenda, you are smart. You can learn anything you put your mind to. And I'm glad you're in my class." These words were like water to my soul. Every day she built me up with words of life that lifted me like a kite.

Under Mrs. Pentecost's loving care, my broken wings were mended. With her encouragement and support, I even won a citywide art contest. Today, in addition to my other work, I am an accomplished artist.

Her words made me believe I could do anything! Mrs. Pentecost will always have a special place in my heart as the teacher who had the most profound impact on me. She saw the diamond in me.

She was a godsend. To this day, I tear up when thinking of Mrs. Pentecost. I know she was my angel who came into my life to help me get my wings back.

I share this story with you to illustrate the difference between a *Dream Buster* and a *Dream Builder.* Dream Busters are those who see you more like a piece of coal. They don't believe in you enough to speak words of life to build your confidence as you pursue your dreams and goals in life. Instead, their words are destructive, critical, judgmental, and negative, saying things like, "You'll never be able to do that," "You're not smart enough to do that," or "You don't have what it takes." "It's too late for you to do that now."

Dream Builders, on the other hand, are those who see you as a potential diamond or a "diamond in the rough." They believe in your gifts, talents, and dreams enough to push you toward your destiny with words like, "You can do it," "I believe in you," "I support you," "Don't give up," "Keep trying," and "I'm proud of you." Encouragement is oxygen to the soul. Consistent words of life have the power to breathe life and hope in a way that really helps others to see the diamond in themselves.

Maybe you had a Dream Buster, like my original first grade teacher. Perhaps you've been told negative things. I believe we've all encountered Dream Busters to some degree.

Taking the Cuffs Off

If you have never had handcuffs on, you can imagine how it feels. Embarrassment, shame, and loss of respect are just a few of the feelings often associated with this experience. However, it is what handcuffs symbolize that can hurt even worse. These metal arm holders symbolize bondage, confinement, and loss of control. While many people have never had *handcuffs* on, there are those who walk around everyday with *heartcuffs* and *headcuffs* on. *Heartcuffs* means being bound and controlled emotionally due to coming in contact with Dream Busters.

Emotionally wearing *heartcuffs* can be a self-protecting way to keep from being hurt again. It is a coping mechanism that causes people to sometimes close their heart to potential Dream Builders. *Head cuffs* means being bound and controlled mentally by negative thoughts and view of one's self. Many struggle with having a negative view of themselves due to believing lies about them. A mental stronghold means believing something that is not true such as believing one is worthless.

Discovering your greatness means making a decision to take these *heartcuffs* and *headcuffs* off. It means realizing that you have the power to change your view of self and the power to be emotionally healthy so that you can develop into the person God created you to be.

Four Powerful Words

You're not just reading this book for the sake of reading it. This chapter is vital to you if you are still struggling with the emotional and psychological affects of hearing harsh words in your life. As I shared with you earlier, your mouth will only repeat what is received into your brain and ears. If you subject yourself to hearing negative things about yourself, you will begin to believe it.

Maybe you've been treated more like coal than a diamond. Some may not have seen the value in you as a child. Some may not see the value in you even now. Either way, it's okay; as I mentioned before, it didn't kill you. I want you to understand something very important from this day forth about any Dream-Buster words ever spoken to you.

Each of these negative words is a lie! But if deep down you believe it because you've heard it, I want to empower you to get free by using the authority of your mouth to declare the truth. Remember, only truth can cancel a lie.

For years I've had a burning passion to empower people to know how to handle Dream Busters and receive Dream Builders. I know it is part of my destiny; my deep desire is to see others set free from the bondage of negative spoken words. Here's a simple yet powerful response for whenever you come up against a Dream Buster from now on. Just look that person in the eye and respond with these four words: *"I don't receive that."*

Stating these four words will empower you beyond what you ever thought. This will absolutely block the negative words from entering you. It will give you power to reject negativity in a way that is emotionally and mentally healthy. These words will literally just go over your head instead of getting on the inside of you. For example, if someone says to you, "You'll never be able to own your own business," without getting into an argument or debate, simply respond with, "I don't receive that." Saying this will throw the person completely off guard. I have taught this simple concept for several years. Overwhelmingly, many have shared with me how life changing it was to learn a practical way to block negativity from entering their spirit.

Just remember, you do not have to receive everything someone tells you, especially if it is negative. By saying this, your brain and ears will not internalize what was said and, therefore, you will be preventing the poison of negativity from contaminating you.

As this is an interactive book written to have a life-changing impact
on you, if you need to get free from Dream-Buster lies that have plagued you, say the following affirmation in the mirror: *From this day forth, I cancel every lie that has ever been spoken to me such as* [name the dream buster words]. *The truth is, I am highly valued with a purpose and destiny. My gifts and talents make me unique. It's true! Greatness is in me! I will become who I was born to be!*

Letting Life Words In

Just as it took time for you to fully believe negative things about life, it will take time for you to fully believe the positive. But it works! Be consistent with speaking words of life that will change your thinking. When you change your words, you can change your life.

Anyone who has ever been a Dream Buster in your life does not have the final word. You have power to change the course of the rest of your life by speaking words of life.

Now as your life coach, I want you to open your heart as I speak words of life over you right now. As you say these words aloud, your brain and ears will be storing them on the inside of you. Here we go:

You are more than a conqueror! You are an overcomer! Everything you've ever gone through in your life is for a purpose. Your life counts! God has a divine plan for your life. Your dreams will come to pass. You will do great things using your own gifts and talents.

Now I want you to say these four words aloud: "I receive every word." I want you to practice responding every time someone encourages or compliments you by simply saying, "Thank you, I receive that." Many people, especially women, have a hard time accepting compliments because of various insecurities. But if you practice receiving it as well as practice encouraging yourself, it will enhance your life dramatically.

Trust me, every single time you speak and receive these life-giving words into your spirit, it's like having fresh water renew you on the inside. It's also like taking vitamins to build your confidence and your faith that good things are coming forth in your life.

What you speak about you bring about. You draw those very things to you that you talk about. Saying things like "I don't think I can do it", "It's too hard" or "I'll never be able to accomplish that" will shatter your self-confidence. Instead, speak words like "I CAN do it", "I'm well able to do anything I set my mind to", or "I WILL accomplish my goals". In other words, speak into existence the things that you desire to happen rather than what you're experiencing right now. It's powerful, and it works. Life and death are indeed in the power of the tongue, therefore, choose to speak life with each new day.

A Harvest Your Heart Desires

While you strive to live your best life, look around for opportunities to make a positive difference in someone else's life. Whether it's your family member, friend, or co-worker, be ready to deposit into them words that encourage, strengthen, and empower. In other words, speak life to those who are in your life.

There are probably more people in your life that struggle with issues of self-doubt, insecurities, and low self-esteem than you realize. You can make a difference just by speaking words of life to them. Start today intentionally looking for opportunities to be an edifier (one who builds others up). I started several years ago the daily practice of complimenting at least three people everyday. I've heard it said that it takes four compliments to erase one criticism someone has received. If this is the case, we all need to be more careful of what we say to each other and, instead, speak more positive words of affirmation.

It's like sowing seeds. I'm sure you've heard the saying, "What goes around comes around." It's true. Whatever you plant will come back to you, whether good or bad. For example, if you plant an apple seed, eventually an apple tree full of delicious apples will grow up. Likewise, if you plant seeds of encouragement, compliments, love, and generosity, in time you will reap a good harvest. If it doesn't seem you receive enough of these things for yourself, you just need to start sowing some good seeds. It'll come back to you later. To help you get in the mindset of doing this, start saying the following on a regular basis:

I'm good to people and people are good to me. I sow good seeds, and I reap a good harvest.

I can tell you that I speak this affirmation almost every single day, and I see the results of being consistent with it. As you condition yourself to release out of your mouth that you are good to people, it will help you to consciously give the best of yourself to others. *Doing* good and *being* good to others will definitely pay off in so many ways you can't even imagine. Every seed will come back to you multiplied.

Speaking words of life truly works; you're feeding your spirit the right message to help you consciously remember how you treat others. Be the Dream Builder that sows seeds of hope and encouragement into the lives of others. The seeds you sow will definitely bring a harvest later. The most important point for you to remember about this chapter is that words have tremendous power. When you speak of yourself and those around you, purpose in your heart to speak life-filled words that bring about the harvest your heart desires.

BRENDA L. CALDWELL, PH.D.

CHAPTER 5

MAKING YOUR LIFE COUNT BY THE POWER
OF YOUR IMPACT

If you've ever prepared for a job interview, then most likely you've heard to "dress to impress" or that "you don't get a second chance to make a first impression." These catchy phrases are born out of a mold of thinking concerning how our society views outer clothing verses inner clothing. Another way of saying this is outer appearances verses inner character. In today's society, many people strive to have a big house, luxury car, fancy job title, designer clothes, and anything else that will *impress* others. But circumstances of life can cause every material pleasure to be lost overnight.

Webster defines the word *impact* as "a forcible touch." The underlying meaning of impacting others verses impressing others is how forcible or lasting one's touch is. In the example of a job interview, a person who is well dressed and communicates well might be very impressive momentarily to an interviewer.

But when the interviewer meets the next job candidate, this person may be dressed even better, communicate even better, and have more experience, so now he or she has suddenly out-impressed the first job candidate.

Impressing others is based on instant, surface appearances that sometimes fail to pan out due to a change in circumstances or conditions; however, if you have an impact on a person, he or she will not forget you—no matter what. Impacting others leaves them with a lasting, forcible touch.

It means that no matter how much time goes by, whatever impacted them is still making a difference. Think about it for a moment. Who has had the greatest impact on your life and why?_____

_____

_____

_____

_____

_____

_____

_____

_____

Would you like to have the same kind of impact on someone's life? If so, what are you doing right now to make sure this happens? Remember, it won't just happen.

Ask yourself these thought provoking questions: *Who am I impacting right now? Whose life is better because of me? What difference has it made that someone met me?*

The Impact of One Life

It is vital that you think about the impact that you want to make on others. Realizing your greatness is maximizing your ability to influence someone else. When I think of people who have had the most impact on my life, I must first say my mother. Raising six children and four grandchildren on her own, my mother has always stood out to me as a woman of strength, love, and faith. To watch her take care of her family by doing whatever honest work she could has impacted me to have a work ethic, concern for others, integrity, and persevering spirit.

I believe she received these qualities from my late grandfather, Lyles Caldwell, Sr., who definitely instilled these character traits in all of his children and grandchildren as the patriarch of the Caldwell family. He was known for his love for God, his family, and for having a profound work ethic. In fact, he had just pulled into the gas station on his way to work when he fell dead at age eighty-five. Affectionately known as "Dad," my grandfather instilled values in me that truly helped shape my life.

Dr. Martin Luther King, Jr., is another person who has had the most impact on my life. Ever since I was a young girl, I could quote his speeches by heart. In fact, my mother would often tell me that I would be a speaker one day. She would jokingly say, "You don't sound quite as good as Dr. King, but you speak real good."

Studying his life has always fascinated me because of the impact that he made as a leader. Dr. King knew his divine purpose and walked out his destiny as a servant of God called to be a voice of healing, hope, and equality for all. For this reason, I believe one of the main reasons he is celebrated every year is because of the impact his life had on our country.

One person who had a tremendous impact on my life as a mentor is Barbara Green. I met Barbara at one of the first national conferences I had an opportunity to speak at. She was also a speaker at the conference. At the end of my workshop, she shared with me that God told her to invest her time, money, and energy to help develop me. Though she and I live in different states, for the next six years, Barbara did exactly that. I will forever be grateful for the positive impact she made on my life professionally and personally.

Purposeful vs. Passive Impact

There are two kinds of impacts: passive and purposeful. *Passive* impact is living a passive lifestyle without consideration of how you are affecting those who are watching you. This can have a negative or positive affect on someone. A person who uses profanity can influence others to do the same. A parent who smokes can influence their children to become smokers just by exposing them to this habit. On the other hand, a child could be influenced in a positive way by observing their parent showing kindness toward others, even though their parent was not trying to teach them to do the same. So, passive impact is not bad. It's just important to realize that someone is watching you and will be impacted by your actions—be it for good or for bad.

Purposeful impact is intentionally living in such a way that your actions have a positive influence on someone else. Parents who consciously spend time helping their children with homework during their early years are instilling in them that education is important.

Parents who take their children to church on a regular basis are teaching them that religious beliefs are important. When the children grow up, they will be impacted by the foundation of their childhood exposure to church and parental involvement in their schoolwork. Another example of purposeful impact is when you intentionally make time for your friends and family to do fun things. This teaches the importance of having balance in life.

Purposeful impact also means handling your life like it's a diamond. You should ask yourself these two questions, "How am I touching those around me?" and "How do I make others better?" It doesn't matter who you are or how old you are. If you're old enough to read this book, you're old enough to impact someone's life.

Character Impact

Remember: your impact is influenced by your character. I have heard it said that who you are when no one is looking is who you really are. Character is made up of the distinctive qualities that make you who you are. Your character will be noticed even when you don't think someone else is watching. If you want to have a positive impact on those within your sphere of influence, always pay attention to your conversations and your actions.

The word *paramour* is sometimes used in court proceedings involving a divorce. A paramour is a person who is involved in an affair with someone who is married. This person's willingness to participate in such behavior speaks volumes about his/her character. Obviously, this person sees him/herself more as a piece of charcoal. A paramour does not realize his/her true value and worth, thus, settles for charcoal treatment. On the contrary, a *paragon* is a person of high quality and excellence of character. It is also a word that describes a 100-karat, perfect cut diamond of the highest quality. A paragon realizes his/her worth and chooses to exhibit character of the highest quality. Determine in your spirit to be a paragon rather than a paramour as it relates to your own character.

Make a habit of consciously displaying behavior that reflects excellence, whether you feel like it or not. What you say and how you act in every circumstance of your life is definitely going to impact someone else. At home, work, school, church, family gatherings, fellowships with friends, and in other circles of influence, *someone is indeed watching you.* Developing character is a definite prerequisite to discovering greatness within you.

Impacting Family and Friends

Snapping at loved loves or being short-fused is not good and leaves a wound that can cause walls to go up among family members stemming from mistreatment. If you've been guilty of treating others with more patience, tolerance, and kindness than your own family members, start practicing today being sensitive to *what* you say, *how* you say it, and what you do when interacting. It's amazing how sometimes, because we are so comfortable with our family, we don't show the patience or kindness toward them that we would a stranger. In fact, if we're not conscious of our conversation and actions, we will treat others better than our own family.

How you live before your family and friends will definitely have an impact. Remember: to have a purposeful impact, it is important that you consciously look for intentional ways to have a positive influence. Make a habit of doing something kind for your family and friends on a regular basis, no matter how small it is. A phone call, a note of encouragement, or a listening ear will go a long way.

You can make an impact by helping in time of need, expressing love as well as showing love, spending quality time, eating meals together, and having weekly "share" time or monthly "gatherings". Instead of waiting for holidays, birthdays, and anniversaries, start doing little things or giving a "just because I love you" gift anytime throughout the year when your loved ones would least expect it. Treating your loved ones like valuable diamonds will definitely establish you as a true paragon. It is also one of the important keys to discovering your true greatness. You will become highly respected by those who know you best.

Look for Diamond Friends

Friendship is a gift that should be cherished and nurtured. If you desire to have *diamond* friends, ask God to bless you. Even if you were hurt or betrayed in the past by friends, don't let that stop you from opening your heart to someone whom God wants to bring into your life. Start intentionally by being friendly to others wherever you go. Don't be afraid to speak to people first. Strike up a conversation. Showing interest in others is always a good way to get to know people. Look for the diamond in others and in doing so, you just might develop a diamond friendship that will become a priceless gem in your life.

Here's a good place for another affirmation. If you desire to have some new divine friendships, start speaking the following on a regular basis until your new friendships come about.

I **am** *a diamond friend and I* **have** *diamond friends. I am a blessing to my friends and my friends are a blessing to me!*

As with any of your friendships, make sure there is mutual positive influence. Diamond friends will always *enhance* each other, *protect* each other, *correct* each other, and *celebrate* each other. As you strive to exemplify the characteristics of a diamond friend, your impact will definitely make a difference in their lives.

Designed to Make a Difference

In the first chapter, I said that regardless of your background, job title, or level of education, *greatness is in you!* You would not have been born if there were no purpose for your life. You've been divinely designed to make a difference in a way that is uniquely you. No one else can be who you were born to be. And no one else can do what you were born to do. As I mentioned before, no one can beat you at being you!

Who you are is unique to what God put in you even before you were
born. Therefore, being uniquely you means that there are certain gifts, talents, ideals, dreams,

concerns, and passions you have that are simply needed to impact the world around you. Even when you don't know it, others are drawing on what is in you.

The media feeds us a daily dose of get-rich quick schemes, beauty secrets to stay young forever, and a ton of other lies to get our money.

Truthfully, it'll never really be about how much money we amass, how good we look, or what we drive; rather, what matters is what we do to make a difference in some way.

Never Underestimate Your Impact

For me, pulling out the diamond in others is my passion. I guess you can say I'm a *diamond finder* because I strive to look for the greatness within each person. I believe in the greatness of your life, and I know that you are alive to make a difference in some way, so I want to encourage you to keep developing your greatness.

Don't underestimate who you are and the power you have to make a difference just by being willing to be yourself and to give of yourself. Someone admires you, someone whom you don't know. Someone is inspired by you, someone whom you haven't met. Someone sees the diamond in you that you don't see in yourself. Your life counts, so don't count yourself out!

Take a moment. Who has had the most positive impact on your life and why?

_____
_____
_____
_____
_____
_____
_____
_____

It's very important to think about how you live and whom you are impacting along the journey of your life. At the end of this journey, you won't
be able to take anything with you, but you can definitely leave something of value by the way you live and give now. Some of the things you have gone through were simply to empower you to bring out the diamond in someone else.

One of the lines from Dr. King's self–written eulogy has always impacted me to think about the influence of my life. "If I can help somebody as I pass along, if I can show somebody he's traveling wrong, if I can teach somebody a word or song, then my living is not in vain." For almost twenty years, I've devoted my life to inspiring young people to become who they were born to be.

As one who doesn't have any biological children, I've been able to pour myself into many youth and young adults along the journey by being a counselor, mentor, coach, and godmother. With so many youth today dealing with issues—abandonment, anger, rejection, and low self-esteem, just to name a few—it's been my sincere passion to instill in them a sense of purpose and destiny.

Be a Dream Builder!

If you want to make a definite impact, please invest in a child, whether you have your own or not. No matter how old or young you are, there is something you can offer a child that may change his or her life. Your time, encouragement, generosity, and love could be just the thing that helps transform them from a piece of coal into, you guessed it, a diamond!

When I think back to all the young people I've had the pleasure of working with, I can't help but think of Kevin Parker. Kevin was a fourteen-year-old worker participating in a summer job program. I had been assigned as his new job counselor. I made a site visit to introduce myself and to find out his goals. When I asked Kevin what he wanted to be when he grew up, his response caught me off guard. First of all, it wasn't the typical sport goal many boys his age aspire to, such as playing pro basketball or football. He answered, "I-I-I-I-I-I-wa-want-to-to-to-to-to-be-be-be-an air-air-line p-p-p-pilot."

Have you ever heard the phrase, "Everything that comes up does not have to come out?" I was thinking, *Son, you probably need to choose something else because of your speech impediment*. But, I'm thankful that I didn't say this. Not wanting to be a dream buster, I said, "Kevin, that's great! You'll need to study really hard in your school and also work to overcome your stuttering so that you'll be able to communicate clearly."

With a big enthusiastic smile, Kevin's response back was clear, "Okay!" With that said, I became his mentor. His first assignment was to read the inspirational book *Gifted Hands* by Dr. Ben Carson. Kevin needed to see that there was another African American male who had to overcome a "stumbling block" in order to step into his destiny. He was required to do an oral report on Dr. Carson's life.

In his report, Kevin shared with me how it inspired him to know that Dr. Carson had overcome a severe condition of dyslexia to become a world-renowned neurosurgeon.

Appreciation Will Come Later

When I first created my own youth program, Kevin was given leadership responsibilities that allowed him to work on his speech impediment. Working closely with him for the next nine years, I watched Kevin overcome the stumbling blocks of teasing, living in poverty, and facing daily peer pressure. At age twenty-four, Kevin was enrolled in an aviation program at his college. About three weeks before he graduated, he came home from college to visit me late one night.

With tears in his eyes, no longer severely stuttering, he began to tell me the impact I had on his life. Kevin wanted me know that I was the first person who didn't laugh when he said he wanted to be an airline pilot. He went on to say that he appreciated being encouraged to work on his speech impediment so that his dream could come true. I was moved to tears also. I thank God that I didn't say what I was thinking the day he first told me his dream. This is another valuable lesson. I can truly say that the outcome of Kevin's life is one of the reasons I'm so passionate about investing in the lives of young people.

Impact of Your Words

Whomever you're investing in right now, just remember that your *words* and *actions* will go a long way and have a far-reaching impact.

Make sure that what you say now is something you will be proud of when someone reminds you of it years from now. It's worth saying again. *Make sure that what you say now is something you will be proud of when someone reminds you of it years from now.*

In the next chapter, I'll share with you how to be the best you can be so that you will be able to ultimately make the most impact with your life.

CHAPTER 6

NO ONE CAN BEAT YOU BEING YOU!

Throughout this book, I've shared some "how-to" nuggets to help you discover your greatness. I didn't just want to write a book for the sake of writing one. For as long as I've been a speaker, my style has always been empowerment. I absolutely love to provide not only inspiration, but also insight that might be life changing in some way. It's the counselor in me. It's the motivator in me. It's the dream builder in me. It's the coach in me. The bottom line is this: it's my style.

I've gone through periods in my life when I compared myself to other people, especially other speakers. I was at a conference in Ohio years ago where several well-known motivational speakers were speaking, one by one, to an audience of 5,000 teenagers. I had been asked to present a workshop for teens on the same day. Only eight kids showed up.

Needless to say, I felt inferior to the speakers that had the huge audiences. Shaking these feelings off for the sake of the youth, I presented in my own interactive style to the best of my ability. Half-way through my workshop, a young man stood up to tell me that my workshop was the best he had attended during the entire conference. Remember how I told you positive words are like water that renews your spirit? That's exactly what this precious young man's words did for me at that moment. It gave me the confidence I needed to just be me.

When I started being called "Dr. B" several years ago, at first I was uncomfortable with it. I didn't want people to think I was being vain. This nickname actually came from Dee Dee Knowles, my long-time "Barnabus." She started calling me this because, as she put it, I help people "be empowered and be inspired." It just caught on. Before I knew it, I became known as "Dr. B." I accepted it as part of the uniqueness of who I am. The truth is that we must develop the confidence to be ourselves despite what people will think.

Don't Compare Yourself!

Even as a first time author, I struggled with how to write this book. For the past three years, almost everywhere I've gone to speak, people have told me told me I should write a book. When I realized it was time, I looked at other books for ideas. It became stressful at times because I didn't see styles that really felt like me. Then it dawned on me to write my book in my *own* style—encouraging, empowering, and interactive, just like my speaking presentations. At that moment, the stress left me. I started focusing on the gift of having this opportunity to encourage you, challenge you, and hopefully inspire you to maximize the greatness within you.

Likewise, I'm sure at some point in your life you've compared yourself to someone else and didn't quite measure up in your own eyes. You may be struggling right now with comparing yourself to others because of their gifts, talents, social status, or for some other reason.

If you're struggling in those areas, let me help free you right now! You weren't born to do the same things as your family members, friends, co-workers, business associates, or anyone else. No one has your exact same fingerprints, dental prints, or gifts and talents.

You were divinely designed with your own gifts, talents and other special abilities that make you who you are. Never compare yourself to anyone else!

You might not be able to speak to large audiences. You might not be
good in business. You might not be good with computers. You might not be good at organizing. But what *are* you good at? I want you to stop right now and write down those things you know you do well. Think about what comes naturally for you.

_____

_____

_____

_____

_____

_____

_____

Don't Live With Regrets

As I said before, no one can beat you at being you. What you have in you is *valuable.* Maybe there's something you've wanted to do for a long time, but you keep putting it off. Don't sit on your gifts, talents, and dreams. Most of all, don't let the grave have them. In other words, don't die without doing the things you have desired to do for a long time. There's a song of regret that is sung by someone almost everyday. *I woulda, I coulda, I shoulda, I almost, but I didn't.* If you don't want to sing this same song later, pursue your dreams *now*!

Here's an assignment for you. Make time to visit a nursing home next week just to talk with a senior citizen about their life. I have no doubt that at least one of the "I shoulda" phrases will come out of their mouth while sharing their stories with you. Following through with this assignment would actually be win/win. How? First of all, you would be sowing a good seed of kindness that will come back to you later in life. Secondly, you would receive more inspiration to pursue those things you desire deep down to do.

Don't wait too late! So many people have wasted their precious time and talents by putting things off that once were dreams in the heart. Whether you decide to visit a nursing home or not, purpose to live your life to the fullest so that at the end you will have no regrets.

Say the following affirmation:
I use my gifts and talents to bless others. I'm a difference maker everyday of my life!

Discover Your Heart's Desire

Lives are waiting to be touched by what you have on the inside of you. If you don't do what you were created to do, then something will always be missing in your life. If you don't know what your purpose is, try answering the following questions: What is our passion?_____

_____

_____

_____

_____

_____

What is the one thing you would be willing to spend eight hours a day doing, even if you never got paid for it?

_____

_____

_____

_____

_____

_____

You have a divine assignment. What you have in you is the answer to a problem. The things that anger, concern or bother you are the very reasons you were created to make a difference, express below what these are. (Note to layout: insert journaling lines)

The answers to these questions, along with the list of your natural gifts and talents, serve to help you discover your divine purpose. Those things that you are passionate about or concerned about are part of God's plan for your life. You were born to make an impact in those areas.

If you already know your purpose but are not living it out daily—it's time. What you have on the inside of you is needed. You were born to do more than just to live, eat, work, and then die. You were born to make your own mark on the world around you.

Just think; wouldn't the world be so much better if we all were doing what we were created to do?

There's something in you that no one else can do. Don't ever stop believing this. No matter how long it takes, develop a "greatness is in me"

belief system. Greatness doesn't mean you have to find a cure for cancer or even become wealthy in business. It simply means that you live a purpose-filled life because you are maximizing your gifts, time, and talents by doing what you were born to do to make the world better.

Remember this: *Purpose produces passion. Passion produces love. Love produces change. When you love what you do, your passion will help to change the world.*

I want you to pause to affirm yourself right now with the following words of life:

*Greatness is in me! I **will** fulfill my purpose and destiny! I might not be there today, but I'm on my way!*

I discussed in the second chapter that becoming a diamond is definitely a process. Coal must be put under extreme heat and pressure in order to give birth to a diamond gemstone.

For me, this process began when I journeyed through a financial wilderness season after taking the leap of faith to enter the professional speaking arena in 1995. Ever since I discovered my motivational gifts working at the telemarketing company, I began to have a deep desire to encourage, inspire, and empower people with words of life.

Three months before I was laid off from my job, I began to sense in my heart that God was leading me to pursue speaking as a career. Since I had already begun to get paid to speak, I felt I would be successful by committing to it full time. I also had some money saved. I sent out 300 brochures. I was really confident that I could make it work.

Don't Throw in the Towel

Eight months into it, I almost starved to death. Few calls were coming in. Rent was due. My car note too. Food was scarce. In fact, I was eating pinto beans about three times a week. Anyone who really knows me knows that I love pinto beans. But not enough to eat them three times a week. During this time in my life, I had to be a on a bean budget to survive.

It was hard many days, wondering how my bills would be paid. I was definitely tapping into God's daily supply of grace and mercy just to have the strength to keep going. Speaking engagements were coming in so slowly that I could have pursued another job. But I knew in my heart that I was supposed to stick it out for some reason.

I can recall a couple of times when I really wanted to give up on this dream. The first time was at the grocery store. I only had $8.23. Standing near the bread aisle, I held a box of crackers in my right hand and a loaf of bread in my left. Since I was already at my spending limit, I had to choose between buying bread or crackers. I didn't have enough money to buy both. The reality of this was overwhelming. I ran out of the store, leaving the items behind in the basket. I almost broke that day. Thank God that a *Dream Builder* friend bought me groceries and gave me a pep talk.

Another time I came close to giving up was when my Jeep, known to my family and friends as "Big Blue," was nearly repossessed. I was three months behind in my payments and the bill collectors were calling back to back, threatening me. I was stressed out. But, by the grace of God, I finally paid it off.

I'm blessed today to own two jeeps. One is named Faith. The other is

named Destiny. I can truly say Rick Warren's book, *Purpose Driven Life*, definitely applies to me. Whenever I'm in either vehicle, it reminds me that I'm driven by *faith* as I move in *destiny*.

Destiny Will Call!

There were times along the way when I definitely felt like an angry piece of coal that wanted the heat turned off me. But deep down, I knew that it was for my *good* and my *growth* and would lead to *great* opportunities in time.

In fact, the first time I received a call to speak out of town for a conference, I was cooking my usual beans. I was so excited to speak to J. Tyler, vice president of programs for WAVE, Inc. in Washington, DC, I let the beans burn on the stove that day. I figured I could buy another bag of beans. In my heart, I just felt like *destiny* had finally called me and I couldn't ask it to hold on, even for a second. The heat no longer mattered.

Today, I'm living my personal dream as a Dream Builder. The seeds my mother planted years ago have brought forth a harvest of opportunity for me to utilize my gifts. She's enjoying the fruits of her labor as she now often travels with me when I speak. I know that I was born to encourage, inspire, and empower others to do what they were born to do. Everything I've gone through in my life has been like coal— worth a whole lot more than I ever thought. And the lessons I've learned along the way are as priceless to me as diamonds!

The same holds true for you. Where you are right now in your life will lead to a priceless payoff. You must prepare yourself for opportunities that are awaiting you. Your dreams and goals won't just show up at your doorstep. They won't fall out the sky. They won't magically appear out of nowhere. As you plan, put forth energy and effort, and "burn some midnight oil," you will make progress toward achieving those things your heart desires. Keep working and keep believing. Opportunities will open up for you in due season.

Bringing the Best Out of You

A diamond is just a rock until it goes through the continuous heating, cutting, and polishing that is necessary to bring forth its high value. In fact, a diamond in the rough can be mistaken for a worthless pebble. But even so, it's a pebble with potential. Potential simply means possible, although not yet actual, or having the capacity to be developed.

This is you! There is so much more on the inside of you. You have the potential to *do* more, *be* more, and *achieve* more than you ever thought possible.

The most important thing to remember is that no one can beat you at being you! You are indeed a one-of-a-kind, unrepeatable miracle, created by God to make your own mark on the world. Again, don't compare yourself to anyone else. You have everything in you to become who you were born to be. Did you really hear with your heart what you just read? You have everything in you to become who you were born to be. It may need to be developed. But it's in you!

Here's another life giving affirmation:
No one can beat me being me! I have my own purpose and destiny!

As your life coach, I want you to do the following: If you haven't done so already, when you finish reading this book, write a list of your goals for the next one to three years. Start with writing one goal you desire to accomplish by this time next year.

Speak to your goals on a weekly basis. Keep them before you so that you won't forget. Set dates for each goal. Always remember that your goal is *what* you want to do. Your objective is *why* you want to do it. This makes you accountable to yourself and to those of us waiting to be blessed by you.

It'll take *faith, focus*, and *footwork* to bring the best out of you. Nothing just happens. You have to *do* something different if you *want* something different. So what is the passion in you that will cause you to go through the heating, cutting, and refining that will bring out the diamond in you?

It's in You!

If it's starting your own business, it's in you. If it's going to college to pursue your degree, it's in you. If it's creating a program that helps your community, it's in you. If it's launching your ministry full time, it's in you. If it's becoming a better parent or spouse, it's in you. If it's to work with children, it's in you. If it's to pursue the career of your dreams, it's in you. If it's becoming an excellent manager of your finances, it's in you. If it's writing a book, it's in you. What is the "it" that's in you? Your great potential!

I want you to pause right now and think about one thing that you desire to do. When you have it in mind, speak it out of your mouth and then say the following: *I will achieve the goal of _____because...it's in me!*

You were born with God-given potential to shine in your own way. You can develop this potential by making time to intentionally work on yourself as well as your goals. Let go of your past mistakes, failures, and setbacks! Time is of the essence. Let nothing stop you! As a diamond, you will shine the brightest when you're in the best setting. Don't run from your gifts. Don't delay using them. Don't underestimate your potential ever again. And don't be afraid to move into your destiny. Be confident in who you are and what you have on the inside that others will value. Expect to live a life that makes a difference! Expect to impact others for the good! Expect greatness to come forth in your life!

If coal could express itself after completing the process of becoming a highly valued jewel, it would most likely say, "Thank you for seeing greatness in me enough to turn me into a diamond.

My Parting Words to You

As your life coach, I want to speak into your life one more time.

Greatness is in you! Destiny is calling you! You will fulfill your purpose in life! You will rise above every setback, disappointment, and painful experience in your life! Your messes will become a message! Your tests will become a testimony! You are more than a conqueror! You will shine as brightly as the diamond you were born to be!

Do you remember what to say at this point? That's right. *I receive every word!*

Never forget the power of your own words. Continue to speak life-giving words over your life whether you *feel* like it or not. Don't doubt who you are and what you have on the inside of you. Your gifts and talents are valuable and needed. Don't sell yourself short! Believe me when I say...greatness is in you!

Thank you for believing in me enough to buy my first book. You've inspired me to develop my gifts to the fullest. *From Charcoal to Diamond: Discover the Greatness in You* was designed to be *compact* and *power-packed* to make an *impact* on your life. If referred to often, it will provide you with a fresh dose of empowerment and inspiration, whenever you need to be reminded of the greatness within you!

ABOUT THE AUTHOR

Dr. Brenda L. Caldwell, fondly known as Dr. B, is a premier empowerment speaker, psychologist, forgiveness coach, ordained minister and author. She is a graduate of the University of Memphis and holds a Ph.D. in Christian Psychology. A native of Memphis, TN, she is CEO/Founder of Dr. Caldwell Empowerment Services and has previously served as empowerment expert for the CBS and ABC television stations in Memphis. In 2015, Dr. Caldwell began a partnership with Jabez House Charity organization in Barbados, serving as therapist and spiritual mentor to provide restoration and healing to women and teen sex workers in need of transformation. She also served five years as a faculty member of the National Youth Professionals Institute in Washington,

D.C. Dr. Caldwell is the founder of two award winning empowerment programs for middle school and high school students. For over 20 years, she has remained one of the most versatile presenters in the country, having an ability to connect equally with adult and youth audiences as she delivers unforgettable messages of HOPE and HEALING! Her new book, **Surgery for the Soul,** is one of the most insightful books ever written on the subject of FORGIVENESS. In addition, Dr. Caldwell created the Surgery the Soul Experience™, a life-changing one day event allowing men, women and teens who are dealing with issues of unforgiveness and other matters of the heart to participate in a unique experience of not only learning **HOW** to forgive and let go of past hurts, but also engage in a therapeutic surgery equal to receiving a "new heart!" Countless individuals and families have benefited from her God-given skill of penetrating the hearts of people in a transformative way. Dr. Caldwell has been called the "Doctor of Hope" for her unique motivational gift and ability to deal with "matters of the heart" in a way that makes a profound impact on the lives of countless people. For more information on her work, go to www.drbempowers.com.

CONTACT INFORMATION

To Book Dr. Brenda L. Caldwell for the following adult or youth related events, go to www.drbempowers.com or call 662-775-0538.

Surgery for the Soul Experience™: Featuring *The Forgiveness Wall*, Surgery for the Soul Experience is a highly impactful one-day experiential experience that first teaches the biblical principles of forgiveness and then engages participants in an unforgettable life altering therapeutic forgiveness "surgery" that frees the soul! Participants learn the "how to" principles of *extending* forgiveness as well as *receiving* forgiveness. This engaging, eye opening experience empowers individuals to receive a "new heart for a new start." Due to the increase of unhealed hurt throughout the world, Surgery for the Soul Experience™ remains in high demand!

Dr. Caldwell presents four customized Surgery for the Soul events to accommodate specific audience needs.
*Surgery for the Soul Experience for Men™
*Surgery for the Soul Experience for Women™
*Surgery for the Soul Experience for Teens™
*Surgery for the Soul Experience for Leaders™

Church Services: As an ordained minister and

evangelist, Dr. Caldwell speaks at church events for men, women, youth, singles as well as for families.

Sought after for her unique experiential style, she delivers anointed transformative truth that ignites lasting change as a vessel of God.

Women's Ministry: Dr. Caldwell delivers anointed, interactive keynotes, retreats, workshops and special events that address women's issues in a way that yields healing, deliverance and wholeness. She has a unique anointing that empowers women to discover their true worth, purpose and potential.

Singles Ministry: Dr. Caldwell delivers anointed, interactive keynotes, retreats, workshops and special events that address the issues of singles who are divorced, widowed or those who have never married. As a happy and whole single, she ministers from experience to help other singles embrace their singleness as a gift.

The Blessing Ceremony: The Blessing Ceremony is a 60-90 minute special ceremony conducted corporately for churches or for individual families desiring to release a biblical blessing upon loved ones that empowers him or her to prosper in every area of life (spiritually, mentally, emotionally, financially, economically and socially). This is a ceremony that also strengthens the bond and relationships of family members.

Empowerment Coaching/Counseling:

Dr. Caldwell provides one-on-one coaching and world-wide counseling services to promote positive change in clients. Specializing in matters of the heart, she conducts individual and family sessions to affectively address root issues. Dr. Caldwell uses spiritual and practical principles to empower clients to overcome areas of past hurts that may be hindering clients from achieving their goals. She is known for her ability to provide results oriented "how to" steps to enable clients to overcome personal obstacles in pursuit of healing and restoration.

Keynote Speaking:

Dr. Caldwell is a highly requested keynote speaker for conferences, summits, banquets and retreats. Her presence is highly regarded because of her distinctive style that is authentic, alive, thought provoking, compassionate and humorous. She possesses an anointing that captivates and grabs the hearts of audiences from all walks of life.

"There is one ingredient I must have to ensure the success of all my conferences...Dr. B! Enough said." Darrell B. Daniels, Conference Planner, Tampa, FL

<u>Youth Assemblies:</u> Dr. Caldwell partners with middle schools, high schools and youth organizations to provide thought provoking, life altering assembly programs and motivational events to thousands of students each year.

Diplomas Count!™ Assembly Program:

Diplomas Count! is a 90 minute life altering experiential assembly program that ignites hope in the hearts of high school students! It not only addresses the root causes of dropping out, but through engaging and experiential activities, students experience an epiphany that makes them more determined to graduate than ever!

Bully Busters™ Assembly Program:

Bully Busters is a 90 minute assembly program designed to equip middle school and high school students to effectively address issues of bullying with
courage and confidence. Through Dr. Caldwell's unusual ability to connect with the toughest students, bullies often seek to make amends after participating in this experiential assembly that exposes the root causes and effects of bullying.

Diamond Girls™ Assembly Program:

Diamond Girls is a 90 minute assembly program designed to empower and inspire female middle school and high schools to develop healthy self esteem, self worth and healthy peer relationships. In this engaging, experiential and energetic program, female students learn to embrace their commonalities and differences in a way that helps to ignite a change in the culture of the school amongst girls.

DreamReachers™ **Assembly Program:**

DreamReachers Assembly Program for middle school
and high school students, is a high energy, thought provoking assembly program that empowers and inspires students to make right choices in order to fulfill their dreams.

*"Uncommon. Rare. Exceptional. Inspirational. Motivational. Electrifying. Each
word describes Dr. B! Throughout my tenure as a principal, I have never met a speaker who possesses the charisma and innate ability to instill hope in the lives of students. Her ability to connect with students is phenomenal!"*
Abby Robinson, Retired Principal, Forrest City High School-Forrest City, AR

Educational Consulting:

Dr. Caldwell provides culture change consulting to schools as well as in-service training and motivational workshops to empower and inspire educators and faculty members in their work with students. In fact, her events for educators and youth professionals are equal to a B12 shot!

"Within our cadre of experts, Dr. Caldwell stands out because she is imbued with a spirit that is truly awe-inspiring!" J. Tyler-Vice President of Training Services, WAVE, Incorporated-Washington, D.C.

Surgery for the Soul: Healing for the Hurting Heart is one of the most uniquely insightful books ever written on the subject of FORGIVENESS! If you've picked up this book, more than likely you or someone you know needs this eye-opening truth! Do you need to forgive but don't know *how*? Do you need to "let go" of issues from your past but don't know *how*? *Surgery for the Soul: Healing for the Hurting Heart* answers the HOW-TO! Through practical application, this remarkable book reveals the root reasons beneath issues like "Uns" . . . Unhealed hurts, Unresolved issues, and Unmet needs caused by the biggest "Un" of all, Unforgiveness! Father issues, mother issues, abuse, childhood hurt, relationship hurt, rejection abandonment, shame, anger, and betrayal are all matters of the heart that make forgiving hard to do, even for Christians! However, through Dr. Brenda L. Caldwell's interactive role as "spiritual surgeon," readers take an journey to "Mercy Hospital" to experience a therapeutic heart surgery that sets the soul free! Forgiveness is the surgery that heals the heart. Discover how to walk in true forgiveness in a way you never thought possible, and experience the favor of God in every area of your life!

Whether you need to learn how to *extend* forgiveness or to *receive* forgiveness, *Surgery for the Soul: Healing for the Hurting Heart* is anointed to transform your life by giving you a *new heart* for a *new start*! An excellent read for individuals or groups!

FROM CHARCOAL TO DIAMOND

BRENDA L. CALDWELL, PH.D.